HOW TO WRITE A LESSON PLAN

Molly E. Rose

CONTENTS

THIS BELONGS TO:

Name

Room

eMail

Phone

INTRODUCTION

This "How To" book is different.

Unlike every other book you'll read with titles like "How To Craft The Perfect Lesson Plan in 165 Incredibly Simple Steps", this book is different. It's a simple "How To" guide for creating a lesson plan that's right for you and your students and also an easy to follow workbook.

We'll discuss what exactly a lesson plan is and why you even need one. We'll then go on to look at the process for creating a lesson plan, including the questions you need to consider (so that you don't forget anything important!)

Then we've got 60 lesson plan templates for you to follow, with a double-page layout so that you have plenty of space for all your notes. We've even included some 'Further Notes' pages at the back for anything else you need to jot down.

Teaching students of any age is both a challenging and daunting prospect. With a well-thought out lesson plan in place (anticipating the questions you'll face AND the answers) it will be much less daunting and much more exciting.

Good luck!

Molly

WHAT IS A LESSON PLAN?

So, what exactly is a lesson plan and why do you even need one?

In simple terms, a lesson plan is a detailed step-by-step process that covers a number of different aspects of the lesson. These are the lesson objectives (for what students will achieve over the course of the lesson). How the students will learn it (including what you'll tell them and what activities they'll do themselves). What assessment there will be (both in-class work and homework assignments) and, finally, what materials you'll need for class.

Creating a lesson plan involves setting all of these down for you to use before, during, and after class. All the best lesson plans involve a specific process or series of steps and we'll go through these in a moment.

WHY DO YOU NEED ONE?

It's a question that's often asked by people who've never taught before, isn't it?!

Simply put, the lesson plan is there to help guide you through the flow of the lesson and make sure you don't forget anything important. They're essential in case a substitute teacher is needed to take a class. They're also useful when you need to refer back to the same lesson in future.

HOW TO CREATE A LESSON PLAN

When you're creating a lesson plan for students of any age (and for any topic) there are three key aspects that you need to consider. These are:

1. Who your students are (in terms of learning styles, group dynamics, etc)

2. What the objective of the lesson is (what's the point of you and your students being there?)

3. How you're going to allocate lesson time (to make sure you cover everything you need to in the time available)

A good lesson plan should be comprised of the following sections. We'll take a closer look at each of these over the page.

- Key reference information
- The main learning objective
- Materials needed for the class
- Warm-up activities
- Presenting the topic
- Discussion and review activities
- Assessment activities

HOW TO CREATE A

LESSON PLAN (CONT.)

As we've seen, a good lesson plan should be comprised the following sections:

Key reference information — This will include the subject, grade or level, topic, date and time

The main learning objective — The starting point in creating a lesson is to determine what the big idea is behind the lesson

Materials needed — Because it's too easy to forget critical items in the run up to a class!

Warm-up activities — these are games or simple tasks that you'll use to get students ready for learning

Presenting the topic — How you'll introduce the subject matter to them

Discussion/review activities — either the whole class or break-out groups

Assessment activities — either in-class or homework to consolidate learning

Over the page you'll now find **60 double-page templates**, following this process, that you can use to plan your lessons. Enjoy!

Subject

Grade/Level

Topic

Date/Time

Learning objective

Materials needed

Warm-up activities

Presenting the topic

Subject

Grade/Level

Topic

Date/Time

Learning objective

Materials needed

Warm-up activities

Presenting the topic

Subject

Grade/Level

Topic

Date/Time

Learning objective

Materials needed

Warm-up activities

Presenting the topic

Subject

Grade/Level

Topic

Date/Time

Learning objective

Materials needed

Warm-up activities

Presenting the topic

Subject	Grade/Level
Topic	Date/Time

Learning objective

Materials needed

Warm-up activities

Presenting the topic

Discussion and review activities

In-class assessment

Homework assignment

Notes

Subject

Grade/Level

Topic

Date/Time

Learning objective

Materials needed

Warm-up activities

Presenting the topic

Discussion and review activities

In-class assessment

Homework assignment

Notes

Discussion and review activities

In-class assessment

Homework assignment

Notes

Subject

Grade/Level

Topic

Date/Time

Learning objective

Materials needed

Warm-up activities

Presenting the topic

Discussion and review activities

In-class assessment

Homework assignment

Notes

Subject

Grade/Level

Topic

Date/Time

Learning objective

Materials needed

Warm-up activities

Presenting the topic

Discussion and review activities

In-class assessment

Homework assignment

Notes

Subject

Grade/Level

Topic

Date/Time

Learning objective

Materials needed

Warm-up activities

Presenting the topic

Discussion and review activities

In-class assessment

Homework assignment

Notes

Discussion and review activities

In-class assessment

Homework assignment

Notes

Subject

Grade/Level

Topic

Date/Time

Learning objective

Materials needed

Warm-up activities

Presenting the topic

Discussion and review activities

In-class assessment

Homework assignment

Notes

Subject	Grade/Level
Topic	Date/Time

Learning objective

Materials needed

Warm-up activities

Presenting the topic

Subject

Grade/Level

Topic

Date/Time

Learning objective

Materials needed

Warm-up activities

Presenting the topic

Discussion and review activities

In-class assessment

Homework assignment

Notes

Subject

Grade/Level

Topic

Date/Time

Learning objective

Materials needed

Warm-up activities

Presenting the topic

Discussion and review activities

In-class assessment

Homework assignment

Notes

Discussion and review activities

In-class assessment

Homework assignment

Notes

Subject

Grade/Level

Topic

Date/Time

Learning objective

Materials needed

Warm-up activities

Presenting the topic

Discussion and review activities

In-class assessment

Homework assignment

Notes

Subject

Grade/Level

Topic

Date/Time

Learning objective

Materials needed

Warm-up activities

Presenting the topic

Discussion and review activities

In-class assessment

Homework assignment

Notes

Subject

Grade/Level

Topic

Date/Time

Learning objective

Materials needed

Warm-up activities

Presenting the topic

Discussion and review activities

In-class assessment

Homework assignment

Notes

Discussion and review activities

In-class assessment

Homework assignment

Notes

Subject

Grade/Level

Topic

Date/Time

Learning objective

Materials needed

Warm-up activities

Presenting the topic

Discussion and review activities

In-class assessment

Homework assignment

Notes

Subject

Grade/Level

Topic

Date/Time

Learning objective

Materials needed

Warm-up activities

Presenting the topic

Subject	Grade/Level

Topic	Date/Time

Learning objective

Materials needed

Warm-up activities

Presenting the topic

Subject

Grade/Level

Topic

Date/Time

Learning objective

Materials needed

Warm-up activities

Presenting the topic

Discussion and review activities

In-class assessment

Homework assignment

Notes

Subject

Grade/Level

Topic

Date/Time

Learning objective

Materials needed

Warm-up activities

Presenting the topic

Discussion and review activities

In-class assessment

Homework assignment

Notes

Discussion and review activities

In-class assessment

Homework assignment

Notes

Subject

Grade/Level

Topic

Date/Time

Learning objective

Materials needed

Warm-up activities

Presenting the topic

Discussion and review activities

In-class assessment

Homework assignment

Notes

Subject

Grade/Level

Topic

Date/Time

Learning objective

Materials needed

Warm-up activities

Presenting the topic

Discussion and review activities

In-class assessment

Homework assignment

Notes

Subject

Grade/Level

Topic

Date/Time

Learning objective

Materials needed

Warm-up activities

Presenting the topic

Discussion and review activities

In-class assessment

Homework assignment

Notes

Discussion and review activities

In-class assessment

Homework assignment

Notes

Subject

Grade/Level

Topic

Date/Time

Learning objective

Materials needed

Warm-up activities

Presenting the topic

Discussion and review activities

In-class assessment

Homework assignment

Notes

Subject

Grade/Level

Topic

Date/Time

Learning objective

Materials needed

Warm-up activities

Presenting the topic

Subject

Grade/Level

Topic

Date/Time

Learning objective

Materials needed

Warm-up activities

Presenting the topic

Discussion and review activities

In-class assessment

Homework assignment

Notes

Subject

Grade/Level

Topic

Date/Time

Learning objective

Materials needed

Warm-up activities

Presenting the topic

Discussion and review activities

In-class assessment

Homework assignment

Notes

Discussion and review activities

In-class assessment

Homework assignment

Notes

Subject

Grade/Level

Topic

Date/Time

Learning objective

Materials needed

Warm-up activities

Presenting the topic

Discussion and review activities

In-class assessment

Homework assignment

Notes

Subject

Grade/Level

Topic

Date/Time

Learning objective

Materials needed

Warm-up activities

Presenting the topic

Discussion and review activities

In-class assessment

Homework assignment

Notes

Subject

Grade/Level

Topic

Date/Time

Learning objective

Materials needed

Warm-up activities

Presenting the topic

Discussion and review activities

In-class assessment

Homework assignment

Notes

Discussion and review activities

In-class assessment

Homework assignment

Notes

Subject

Grade/Level

Topic

Date/Time

Learning objective

Materials needed

Warm-up activities

Presenting the topic

Discussion and review activities

In-class assessment

Homework assignment

Notes

Subject

Grade/Level

Topic

Date/Time

Learning objective

Materials needed

Warm-up activities

Presenting the topic

Subject	Grade/Level

Topic	Date/Time

Learning objective

Materials needed

Warm-up activities

Presenting the topic

Subject

Grade/Level

Topic

Date/Time

Learning objective

Materials needed

Warm-up activities

Presenting the topic

Subject

Grade/Level

Topic

Date/Time

Learning objective

Materials needed

Warm-up activities

Presenting the topic

Subject

Grade/Level

Topic

Date/Time

Learning objective

Materials needed

Warm-up activities

Presenting the topic

Discussion and review activities

In-class assessment

Homework assignment

Notes

Subject	Grade/Level
Topic	Date/Time

Learning objective

Materials needed

Warm-up activities

Presenting the topic

Discussion and review activities

In-class assessment

Homework assignment

Notes

Discussion and review activities

In-class assessment

Homework assignment

Notes

Subject

Grade/Level

Topic

Date/Time

Learning objective

Materials needed

Warm-up activities

Presenting the topic

Discussion and review activities

In-class assessment

Homework assignment

Notes

Subject

Grade/Level

Topic

Date/Time

Learning objective

Materials needed

Warm-up activities

Presenting the topic

Discussion and review activities

In-class assessment

Homework assignment

Notes

Subject

Grade/Level

Topic

Date/Time

Learning objective

Materials needed

Warm-up activities

Presenting the topic

Discussion and review activities

In-class assessment

Homework assignment

Notes

Discussion and review activities

In-class assessment

Homework assignment

Notes

Subject

Grade/Level

Topic

Date/Time

Learning objective

Materials needed

Warm-up activities

Presenting the topic

Discussion and review activities

In-class assessment

Homework assignment

Notes

Subject

Grade/Level

Topic

Date/Time

Learning objective

Materials needed

Warm-up activities

Presenting the topic

Subject

Grade/Level

Topic

Date/Time

Learning objective

Materials needed

Warm-up activities

Presenting the topic

Discussion and review activities

In-class assessment

Homework assignment

Notes

Subject

Grade/Level

Topic

Date/Time

Learning objective

Materials needed

Warm-up activities

Presenting the topic

Discussion and review activities

In-class assessment

Homework assignment

Notes

Discussion and review activities

In-class assessment

Homework assignment

Notes

Subject

Grade/Level

Topic

Date/Time

Learning objective

Materials needed

Warm-up activities

Presenting the topic

Discussion and review activities

In-class assessment

Homework assignment

Notes

Subject

Grade/Level

Topic

Date/Time

Learning objective

Materials needed

Warm-up activities

Presenting the topic

Discussion and review activities

In-class assessment

Homework assignment

Notes

Subject

Grade/Level

Topic

Date/Time

Learning objective

Materials needed

Warm-up activities

Presenting the topic

Discussion and review activities

In-class assessment

Homework assignment

Notes

Discussion and review activities

In-class assessment

Homework assignment

Notes

Subject

Grade/Level

Topic

Date/Time

Learning objective

Materials needed

Warm-up activities

Presenting the topic

Discussion and review activities

In-class assessment

Homework assignment

Notes

Subject

Grade/Level

Topic

Date/Time

Learning objective

Materials needed

Warm-up activities

Presenting the topic

Subject

Grade/Level

Topic

Date/Time

Learning objective

Materials needed

Warm-up activities

Presenting the topic

Subject

Grade/Level

Topic

Date/Time

Learning objective

Materials needed

Warm-up activities

Presenting the topic

Discussion and review activities

In-class assessment

Homework assignment

Notes

Subject

Grade/Level

Topic

Date/Time

Learning objective

Materials needed

Warm-up activities

Presenting the topic

Discussion and review activities

In-class assessment

Homework assignment

Notes

Discussion and review activities

In-class assessment

Homework assignment

Notes

Subject

Grade/Level

Topic

Date/Time

Learning objective

Materials needed

Warm-up activities

Presenting the topic

Discussion and review activities

In-class assessment

Homework assignment

Notes

Subject

Grade/Level

Topic

Date/Time

Learning objective

Materials needed

Warm-up activities

Presenting the topic

Discussion and review activities

In-class assessment

Homework assignment

Notes

Subject

Grade/Level

Topic

Date/Time

Learning objective

Materials needed

Warm-up activities

Presenting the topic

Discussion and review activities

In-class assessment

Homework assignment

Notes

Discussion and review activities

In-class assessment

Homework assignment

Notes

Subject

Grade/Level

Topic

Date/Time

Learning objective

Materials needed

Warm-up activities

Presenting the topic

Discussion and review activities

In-class assessment

Homework assignment

Notes

Subject

Grade/Level

Topic

Date/Time

Learning objective

Materials needed

Warm-up activities

Presenting the topic

Subject

Grade/Level

Topic

Date/Time

Learning objective

Materials needed

Warm-up activities

Presenting the topic

Discussion and review activities

In-class assessment

Homework assignment

Notes

Subject

Grade/Level

Topic

Date/Time

Learning objective

Materials needed

Warm-up activities

Presenting the topic

Discussion and review activities

In-class assessment

Homework assignment

Notes

Discussion and review activities

In-class assessment

Homework assignment

Notes

Subject

Grade/Level

Topic

Date/Time

Learning objective

Materials needed

Warm-up activities

Presenting the topic

FURTHER NOTES

FURTHER NOTES

FURTHER NOTES

Made in United States
North Haven, CT
11 April 2022

18124935R00072